AF679297

PUNCHING
ABOVE YOUR WEIGHT

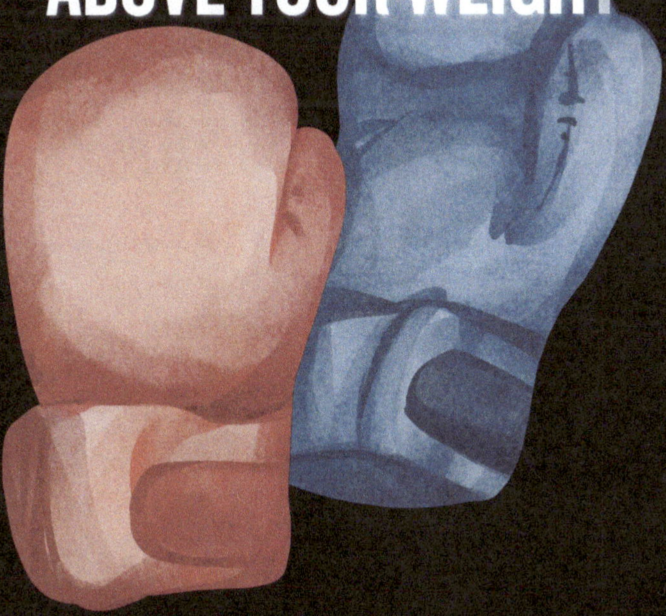

HOW TO USE AI
WITHOUT LOSING YOUR MIND

RYAN J. SMITH

© 2025 Ryan J. Smith

THE STACK PRESS

All rights reserved.

No part of this publication may be copied, stored, or shared without the author's written permission, except for brief quotations used in reviews or commentary.

This is a work of nonfiction. Real experiences, real tools, real results.

ryanjeffreysmith.com

www.graindata.ai

First Edition - 2025

TABLE OF CONTENTS

For my amazing wife and life partner,

Simone Chagoya

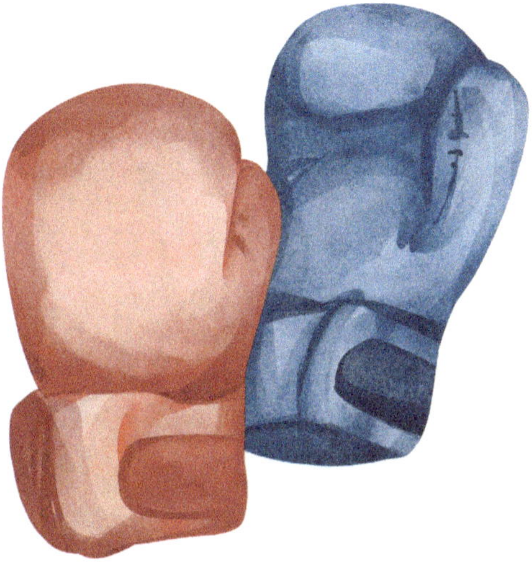

PUNCHING ABOVE YOUR WEIGHT

PREFACE
The Morning After

I finished the first full draft of this book on Memorial Day weekend 2025.

Wrote like I was on fire. Barely slept.

Chased every thread of clarity I could find in a world drowning in noise.

And the next morning, I got the call.

My dad's heart had stopped.

Fifteen minutes.

Flatlined.

He was unconscious, on a ventilator, sedated, and unresponsive.

The doctors didn't know if he'd wake up.

They didn't know if he'd come back.

So I did what I've always done when the world swings.

I braced my stance, and I stayed present.

Because this book is about exactly that:

How to fight when the odds aren't in your favor.

How to move when the machines move faster.

How to think clearly when the system overwhelms.

How to protect your signal when everything tries to blur it.

My dad fought harder than I've ever seen anyone fight.

He flatlined – and then he came back.

Breathing on his own.

Talking.

Fully present.

A miracle, the nurse said.

It reminded me why I wrote this in the first place.

Not to chase trends or decode tech.

But to show you how to punch above your weight – and stay standing.

Even when the lights flicker. Even when the bell feels final.

This isn't a book about AI.

It's a book about staying human in the age of acceleration.

If you're reading this, you're still in the fight.

Let's begin.

– Ryan J. Smith

INTRODUCTION

Fight Smarter

Boxing was the first sport I ever loved.

Not because of the blood or the violence.

Because of the precision.

They call it the *sweet science* for a reason –

It's not about brute force.

It's about leverage. Rhythm. Anticipation.

It's about seeing three moves ahead and taking none for granted.

Every jab is data. Every round is adaptation.

You win not by being the strongest –

You win by being the smartest in the ring.

That mindset clicked for me early.

I grew up watching Tyson fights with my dad – those brutal, blink-and-it's-over knockouts.

But **our hero was always Ali.**

He wasn't just a fighter. He was a strategist.

He moved with conviction. He talked like a poet.

He made you believe that **heart** and **intelligence** could beat raw power.

That if you knew who you were – and stayed in rhythm – you could take on giants.

That belief shaped how I saw the world.

And long before I ever stepped into a boardroom, I learned how to hold my ground.

Years later, after earning a certificate from MIT in Building AI Products & Services and leading AI product work at a $20B healthcare company, I found myself in a different kind of fight.

In corporate meetings, I watched smart, steady professionals grow anxious.

Around the holiday dinner table, relatives didn't ask about AI out of curiosity – but out of *fear.*

...what happens to me if AI takes over?

...what happens to my job?

...how do I keep up?

What I've learned is this: most people aren't afraid of work.

They're afraid of being left behind.

Afraid of becoming irrelevant.

And the truth is, most AI advice isn't written for them – it's written *by* and *for* people who've already made it.

So I wrote this book for the rest of us.

Not a promise. Not a hack.

A **guide**. A way to fight smarter in a world that's moving faster than ever.

You'll learn how to:

- **Use AI** to multiply your output without multiplying your stress
- **Build workflows** that give you back your time
- **Navigate this new era** with structure, clarity, and purpose

You'll also hear from the voices that shaped how I think - not just tech titans and CEOs, but organizers, artists, and writers.

Most of the quotes in this book come from women and people of color.

Not by accident.

Because power hits different when you're not the one holding the mic.

And wisdom from the margins has always existed - we're just finally listening.

I keep a pair of autographed Ali and Frazier gloves on the tallest shelf in my studio. That's where a champion's fists go after the final round. Victory, earned.

If you've ever felt underestimated, overlooked, or outmatched – this is your corner.

I won't promise it'll be easy.

But you've already got the grit. The instincts.

The **fight.**

Now it's time to sharpen your stance, tighten your form, and step back into the ring.

Let's go.

Hype Music for the Underdog

Every round in this book includes a hype track – songs that carried me through hard days and big swings. Think of it as entrance music for the underdog.

Before every fight, you need *rhythm.* A pulse. A voice louder than the noise.

Some songs are fire.

Some are water.

All of them helped me stay upright. Expect some surprises.

- For Round 1, it's "UNDERDOG" BY SLY & THE FAMILY STONE – because owning your story is the first punch.
- For the Obama chapter on self-leadership under pressure, it's "A CHANGE IS GONNA COME" BY SAM COOKE – because composure is a kind of resistance.

Let these songs frame the fight. Let them remind you who you are.

Scan here to listen to the soundtrack on Spotify

Use the following framework as a lens.

You'll see traces of it in every round –

whether it's building systems, cutting noise, or staying dangerous.

Let it guide your fight.

FIGHT

FRAMEWORK

FORM YOUR STANCE

You can't outrun chaos if you don't know your center.
Root down. Breathe deep. Begin from the truth.

ITERATE WITH LEVERAGE

Don't chase every edge - refine your rhythm.
Build with tools, but shape with taste.

GUARD YOUR FOCUS

Attention is currency.
Protect it like it's sacred - because **it is.**

HARNESS YOUR TEAM

Move like you've got backup - even when you're solo.
Assign the machine. Keep the signal.

TRANSMIT YOUR SIGNAL

When the noise is loud, clarity is rebellion.
Say it sharp. Say it real. Let it echo.

RYAN J. SMITH

ROUND ONE: WAKE UP TO THE FIGHT

This isn't the warm-up. This is round one.

"Only a [person] who knows what it is like to be defeated can reach down to the bottom of their soul and come up with the extra ounce of power it takes to win."

Muhammad Ali

Bell Rings - The Villain Has Entered the Ring

Every era has its villain. A force so unyielding it doesn't knock – it **bursts through the door.**

In ours, it's not a warlord. Not a tyrant.

It's a machine.

Or more precisely: the consequence of many machines learning to think, build, and accelerate –

without permission.

AI is not the villain because it's evil.

It's the villain because it's *relentless.*

It doesn't sleep.

It doesn't second-guess.

It doesn't hesitate.

It rewrites pitch decks at 3 a.m.

Builds strategy docs in seconds.

Summarizes your meeting before you've left the room.

It doesn't wait.

It **acts.**

And you?

You're still waiting for your calendar to open up.

(probably to meet about meetings.)

AI is already punching above your weight.

This book isn't fear.

It's **fight.**

You don't need to out-code it.

But you must *out-clarify* it.

You don't need to beat it.

But you do need to *train with it.*

Learn its rhythm.

Find your stance.

> "You could leave life right now. Let that determine what you do, say, and think."
> Marcus Aurelius

The bell already rang.

You're in the ring.

Let's sharpen your stance.

The Stoic Duality - Train or Fight

No one's coming to tell you when to begin.

Only you can decide when the warm-up ends.

I reread *Meditations* every year.

Not for quotes.

To remember how to breathe.

The Stoics don't offer hacks.

They offer **form.**

Precision.

Timing.

They remind me: there are only two modes –

- ***Train***
- ***Fight***

Most people confuse the two.

They sprint through email.

Bounce between Slack threads and dopamine loops.

Always reacting.

Always flinching.

They mistake motion for progress.

Exhaustion for effort.

But if you're always fighting, you're never training.

And if you're never training, you can't win the fight that matters.

This book is your gym.

You won't leave it with more tasks.

You'll leave it with **clarity.**

Underdog Interlude - Frida Trained in the Margins

At 18, Frida Kahlo's future was obliterated in a bus crash.

Her spine was fractured. Her plans to become a doctor – gone.

Confined to a bed in a plaster corset, she didn't ask for sympathy.

She asked for a mirror... bolted to the ceiling.

And a brush.

She didn't wait for the world to open up.

She made a world inside a frame.

Every stroke was a system.

Every portrait, a prototype of identity.

She didn't create for applause.

She created to survive.

> *"I paint myself because I am so often alone and because I am the subject I know best."*
>
> Frida Kahlo

That's what most people miss about AI:

It's not a replacement for vision.

It's a **mirror.**

A tool to scale what you already know, feel, and fight for.

But only if you've done the inner work first.

Frida didn't wait to be whole.

She trained through pain.

And built a voice no machine could replicate.

That's Round One leverage:

Turning your limits into design constraints.

Turning the margins into momentum.

La Columna Rota,
1944 by Frida Kahlo

This Book Isn't Anti-AI. It's Pro-Agency

I want to be clear: I'm not against AI.

I'm against letting it shape the future without shaping ourselves first.

During my MIT certification in AI product design, I learned about how AI is helping doctors detect and treat breast cancer earlier – saving lives that might've slipped through the cracks. These tools don't just automate. They **amplify.** When used with care, they enhance human insight instead of replacing it.

That's not dystopia. That's design.

The problem isn't AI.

It's how untrained we are to use it well.

If you don't know your own rhythm, you can't lead the dance.

If you don't know your edge, you'll just chase the tool of the week.

This book isn't a doomsday manifesto.

It's a call to sharpen your stance.

Because AI can give you speed –

but only you can bring the signal.

Training Camp - Starting GRAIN in the Margins

When I started building GRAIN, I was already full.

AI Product Manager at a $20B healthcare company.

Managing strategy, delivery, deadlines, politics.

There was no extra room.

So I carved space where I could.

Early mornings. Late nights. Quiet weekends - when most people catch their breath.

That's how GRAIN was born.

Not out of hustle.

Out of **clarity.**

I didn't have a team.

I had workflows.

I didn't have funding.

I had **force.**

I used AI to:

- ***Summarize*** 20-page decks and extract signal from fluff
- ***Prototype*** branding and positioning with rhythm
- ***Build*** landing pages and refine pitch decks while others were still outlining

That's not productivity.

That's **compression.**

Momentum.

Leverage.

Combo Move - Leverage is the New Discipline

Discipline isn't doing more.

That's superstition.

Discipline is knowing what *deserves* your energy -

and building systems for **everything else.**

That's where AI lives:

It won't give you vision.

But it will help you *express* yours.

It won't make your decisions.

But it will clear the noise so you can.

It won't build your dream.

But it will hand you the tools to build faster, stronger, and with less drag.

You don't need to fear being replaced by AI.

You need to fear being **out-leveraged** –

by another **human** using AI with clarity, taste, and intent.

If you're not actively training your stack – your mindset, your process, your edge –

you're not in the fight.

You're watching from the crowd.

"UNDERDOG" BY SLY & THE FAMILY STONE

"I know how it feels to get demoted when it comes time to get promoted."

Sly doesn't ease in – he *launches*. The horns hit. The groove punches.
Before you know it, you're standing straighter.

This is undeniable funk with something to prove.
It's for the fighter who never got the spotlight.
The grinders who kept swinging without applause.

Perfect for Round One – because that's when you decide:
Do you stay on the mat, or pick yourself up?

The beauty of this track is in its refusal to fold.
It doesn't ask for validation.
It **claims space.**

The Finish - Round One Was Never Optional

> "*You have power over your mind – not outside events. Realize this, and you will find strength.*"
> Marcus Aurelius

This is not the warm-up.

This is Round One.

This book isn't permission.

It's a **playbook**.

Every chapter, every prompt, every story –

Pressure-tested. Forged in real-time while building GRAIN.

No theory. Just lived rhythm.

The bell rang.

AI landed the first knockdown.

Are you getting back up?

What critical decision am I postponing - and what would change if I made it today?

Behind the Curtain: *What Makes GPT So Powerful?*

Let's demystify the engine behind the curtain.

You keep hearing about "GPT," "LLMs," "AI tools," and "the algorithm." But what does that actually mean?

GPT stands for **Generative Pretrained Transformer.** It's a type of **large language model** (LLM), which means it's trained to understand and generate human-like text at scale.

And when I say "scale," I mean this thing has digested:

- Billions of words
- Thousands of books
- Countless conversations, codebases, tutorials, product docs, and more

It doesn't "think" like a person.

It predicts.

It sees a sentence like "The sky is..." and calculates – based on everything it's learned – what the next likely word should be.

But here's what makes it powerful:

It doesn't just predict one word.

It predicts the next one, and the next one, and the next - at blistering speed and stunning nuance.

And it doesn't stop at English.

It speaks dozens of languages.

Writes code in multiple programming dialects.

Takes messy thoughts and polishes them into punchy headlines.

Takes vague ideas and scaffolds them into business strategies, product roadmaps, or bedtime stories - depending on your prompt.

But don't let the magic fool you.

GPT isn't conscious.

It isn't wise.

It's not your therapist or your cofounder or your soulmate.

It's a **mirror**, a **mixer**, and a **magnifier**.

It reflects how you think.

It blends what it's seen.

And it amplifies what you ask for.

That's why prompts matter.

That's why **clarity** matters.

And that's why your edge still matters.

The better you train your inputs – your system, your voice, your taste – the more leverage you get from the machine.

You don't need to build the model.

You just need to know how to drive it.

ROUND TWO: KNOW YOUR WEIGHT CLASS

Clarity is your competitive edge.
Fight the right battles.

"I'm not afraid of storms, for I'm learning how to sail my ship."

Louisa May Alcott

Bell Rings - Get Up or Stay Down

You're still on the mat.

Your cheek's against the canvas.

Your breath is sharp.

The world feels heavier than it did a minute ago.

This is the moment between impact and response.

And the first response has to be **internal**.

Because the next round isn't about tools.

It's about who you *actually* are.

You don't get leverage by pretending to be someone else.

You get it by training your **real edge.**

If you're going to scale, you need to know what's *worth scaling.*

You need to know your weight class.

> "First say to yourself what you would be; then do what you have to do."
>
> Epictetus

Underdog Interlude - The Quiet Champion

My dad grew up in rural Jamaica – not the beach-postcard version, but the dirt-road kind.

The kind where opportunity isn't promised. Where you make your own path or get swallowed by someone else's.

At sixteen, he left everything he knew and boarded a flight to Chicago.

No safety net. No family waiting at the gate. Just a dream and a Chicago winter.

He didn't flinch.

He got to work.

Started from the ground floor – literally.

Stocking shelves. Cleaning.

Slinging Chicago-style hot dogs across from Buckingham Fountain.

Carrying weight no one else wanted to carry.

He learned fast. Moved quicker.

Not by trying to become someone else, but by doubling down on who he already was – sharp, steady, observant.

He watched how Americans moved. How they spoke.

He studied the rules, the rhythm, the game.

And then he beat them at it – quietly.

"One one coco full basket."

Jamaican Proverb

(Little by little, the basket gets full.)

That's how he lived.

No shortcuts. No skipping steps.

Just steady effort stacked over time.

He worked his way up, earned his stripes, and eventually started his own business.

Not because someone handed him a blueprint.

Because he built one from scratch.

There was no spotlight. No viral success story.

But if you were paying attention, you saw it:

A man who knew his weight class – and trained until he could own it.

He didn't posture.

He didn't bluff.

He just kept swinging.

You don't have to be loud to be powerful.

You don't have to go viral to matter.

But you do have to know who you are.

And you do have to move like you mean it.

That's how you punch above your weight – without losing your center.

That's how you win your fight.

"THE PAYBACK" BY JAMES BROWN

"I don't know karate, but I know ka-razy."

This track doesn't explode - it *circles.*

It stalks.

James Brown doesn't rush the groove - he *owns* it. He knows exactly what he's worth, and he's not here to prove it to anyone.

That's **weight class awareness.**

This is Round Two energy:

Measured power. Strategic heat.

Revenge through rhythm.

He's not flailing. He's walking you down.

Every hit is a *receipt.*

Training Camp - Clarity Before Complexity

Self-awareness is leverage.

But most people skip it.

They chase tools before truth.

They bolt on someone else's productivity stack – then wonder why nothing sticks.

They scale tasks that were never aligned with their edge to begin with.

Here's what I had to learn the hard way:

You can't outsource your thinking.

You can't automate your way out of confusion.

And you absolutely can't build a meaningful system around an identity you haven't owned yet.

Before anything else, get honest about where your power comes from. Then reinforce it.

Combo Move - Audit the Fighter

There's a simple framework I return to whenever things start slipping:

Energy Map

List four things:

1. What gives you energy
2. What drains it
3. What moves the needle
4. What just keeps you busy

Now draw a line. Everything in boxes 2 and 4? That's your automation target. Your delegation list. Your "not my fight" zone.

Everything in boxes 1 and 3? That's your ring. That's what AI should amplify - not replace.

This isn't introspection.

It's *architecture.*

You're mapping your actual edge.

"Caring for myself is not self-indulgence, it is self-preservation, and that is an act of political warfare."

Audre Lorde

You are not scaling to become a machine.

You're scaling to protect your focus – because your **focus is the asset.**

Underdog Interlude - Fired from a Warehouse, Freed by the Fall

Before I ever scaled a system, I got fired from a warehouse job.

Why?

Because I was caught ghostriding a forklift with a buddy of mine. *(Hope you're doing well, Freddie!)*

It was reckless. **Dumb.** And, in hindsight, revealing.

My wife said it later, and she was right:

"I think you were *trying* to get fired."

At the time, I didn't know how to articulate what I felt - just that I was underleveraged, unseen, and restless. That job didn't ask for my mind or my edge. And I didn't know how to offer it anyway.

I self-sabotaged before anyone could question if I belonged.

And that's the trap.

Sometimes the people with the most potential self-destruct first – not because they don't care, but because deep down, they know they're meant for more and don't know how to find it.

> *"You can fail at what you don't want, so you might as well take a chance on doing what you love."*
> Jim Carrey (on his father)

That job wasn't failure. It was foreshadowing.

Of the fight to come.

Of the edge I had to train.

Of the clarity I'd eventually earn.

I didn't need to ghost-ride forklifts.

I needed to ghostwrite my future – and start showing up like I was built for something more.

Corner Talk - Leverage Lives in the Margins

When I was building GRAIN, I wasn't trying to do everything.

Yes, I can code.

I've built full-stack systems.

But I know where I create the most value.

It's not chasing every edge case.

It's designing the system.

Setting the direction.

Translating complexity into movement.

That was my weight class - and I protected it like a title belt.

AI helped me:

- *Draft value props in multiple voices to test positioning fast*
- *Turn raw notes into decks, landing pages, and strategy docs*
- *Move with rhythm - by letting tools scaffold the work while I focused on the signal*

It wasn't about doing more.

It was about doing the **right things** - with power.

Learn With Me - What AI Can (and Can't) Do Today

Featuring:

Dr. Joy Buolamwini

Founder, **The Algorithmic Justice League**

> *"We cannot fight what we cannot see. And right now, we're still learning to see the full impact of AI."*

AI can do a lot. But it can't do everything. And more importantly - it often doesn't do what it does fairly.

Dr. Joy Buolamwini is a pioneer in the fight for algorithmic justice. She reminds us that AI reflects the data we feed it. If you don't understand what it was trained on - or who was left out - you don't understand what it's likely to do.

This round is about awareness. Your weight class isn't just defined by your tools - but by your ethics, your blind spots, and your ability to sense where AI adds value vs. where it adds bias.

Corner Insight → *Use AI to assist clarity - not to replace responsibility.*

The Finish - Your Edge Is Not Optional

> *"If you are distressed by anything external, the pain is not due to the thing itself, but to your estimate of it."*
> Marcus Aurelius

You don't need to be a generalist.

You need to be a **builder who knows their edge.**

You need to know when to train.

When to strike.

And when to hand the gloves to the system you built.

That starts with owning your strengths.

Your limitations.

Your *rhythm.*

The people who win in this new economy?

They don't try to be everything.

They fight clean.

They fight smart.

And they never step out of their weight class –

without a damn good reason.

If I lost 90% of my work memory,
what 3 tasks would I rebuild first -
and why?

ROUND THREE: TOOLS DON'T WIN FIGHTS

AI is your corner man – not your champion.

"You can't be afraid of what you don't know. That's the edge."

Ava DuVernay

Bell Rings - The Flood Has No Favorites

AI isn't a secret anymore.

Everyone's got the same gear: ChatGPT, Midjourney, Claude, Perplexity, Notion AI.

The toolkit is public.

The pace is relentless.

But here's the truth:

Access isn't the edge. Application is.

And the winners?

They're not just using the tools better.

They're using them with **taste.**

Anyone can generate output.

Few can generate trust, clarity, and direction.

That's the new advantage.

Training Camp - The Illusion of Efficiency

Movement does not equal *momentum.*

We've all seen it:

- Notion dashboards no one opens
- Auto-generated decks that say nothing
- Slack bots that just add noise

It looks slick.

It looks fast.

But it's AI-powered waste.

Tools won't save you.

Taste will.

Taste tells you what not to build.

It strips noise, sharpens signal.

Without it, you're just scaling fluff.

Underdog Interlude - Basquiat Didn't Wait for Permission

Jean-Michel Basquiat never studied design.

He didn't take the "proper" route.

He painted with oil sticks on scrap doors and fridge panels.

He wasn't supposed to belong in galleries.

He wasn't fluent in art theory.

He was fluent in **urgency**.

What he lacked in polish, he made up for in velocity.

Raw lines. Explosive color. Crowned skulls and fractured phrases.

A style born not from tradition – but from pressure.

> *"I don't think about art when I'm working. I try to think about life."*
>
> Jean-Michel Basquiat

Basquiat didn't wait to master the tools.

He made the tools irrelevant.

His edge was taste.

Discernment under fire.

A voice that didn't ask to be translated.

That's the lesson.

It's not about mastering software.

It's about mastering what you stand for.

That's how you punch above your weight:

By making your edges unmistakable –

Even when the world tells you to smooth them out.

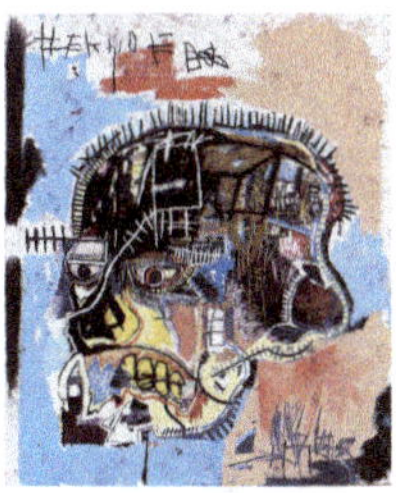

Untitled, 1981

Combo Move - Use AI Like an Artist

Here's the real move:

- I draft 5 headlines in `GPT` - *then trust my gut on the one that lands*
- `Claude` lays out a proposal – *but I shape it like I'm pitching live*
- Image tools spark ideas – *but I define the brand myself*

AI is the brush.
Taste is the hand.

The further you scale, the more your discernment matters.

Because at scale, every decision compounds.

And bad decisions at speed?

That's how things fall apart.

Corner Talk - I Still Make the Call

AI helped shape this book.

It drafted. Remixed. Suggested.

But every time something felt off?

I stepped in.

I re-voiced.

I refined – *obsessively.*

This isn't some auto-generated productivity guide.

This is signal.

This is *voice.*

This is **standard.**

I trust the tools –

Because I *never* trust them blindly.

AI will spit out confident nonsense. Only someone with taste knows the difference.

You lead the system. Or it leads you.

“DNA.” BY KENDRICK LAMAR

"I got power, poison, pain, and joy inside my DNA"

This isn’t just hype. It’s blueprint music.

"DNA." is an x-ray of identity.

It's not about performance. It's about what's already inside you –

whether or not the world sees it yet.

In an era where anyone can generate content, Kendrick reminds us:

What makes you dangerous is your discernment.

Your clarity.

Your taste.

This track doesn't beg for attention.

It commands it.

Every bar is intentional.

Every switch-up is designed.

It's raw precision. Controlled fire.

Because taste isn't something you bolt on after the fact.

It's what defines the entire system.

"I was born like this, since one like this, immaculate conception..."

AI is the brush.

Taste is the hand.

And what's in your hand better match what's in your blood.

That's **DNA.**

The Finish - Scale Is Not Strategy

"Everything we touch, we turn into a weapon."
Angela Davis

The AI flood is rising.

Everyone's sprinting.

Everyone's building.

But not everyone's **thinking.**

Not everyone's **curating.**

Not everyone's **editing.**

And that's where you win.

You don't need 100 tools.

You need 3 that multiply your **taste.**

Because tools don't make you better.

They make you *more* of what you already are.

What am I scaling that I haven't actually vetted?

ROUND FOUR: DESIGN FOR LEVERAGE

Build systems that scale you, not systems you scale.

"You have to be a little bit of a hustler, a little bit of a street fighter, and a little bit of a philosopher."

Anthony Bourdain

Bell Rings - Stop Trying to Do More

Let's get something straight:

You're not tired because you're lazy.

You're tired because your system is broken.

You wake up already behind.

You finish the day with a list that grew longer – not shorter.

You're still trying to white-knuckle your way through a world that rewards **precision over effort.**

That's not a motivation problem.

That's a design problem.

You don't need another productivity hack.

You need a system that throws punches while you sleep.

Here's the secret: **A great system is a silent assassin.**

It works while you breathe. *It builds whether or not you're watching.*

Training Camp - What Most People Get Wrong About Systems

Everyone talks about systems.

Very few actually build them.

They confuse a system with a pretty dashboard, a color-coded map, a Notion board they never open.

But real systems?

- Reduce decision fatigue
- Eliminate wasted motion
- Trigger momentum
- Compress time
- Protect your edge

Most of all? They **multiply force.**

You don't earn leverage by sprinting.

You earn it by building once – so it hits *forever.*

Underdog Interlude - Temple Grandin Saw Systems in the Chaos

Temple Grandin didn't speak until she was four.

She was told she wouldn't amount to anything.

Too odd. Too sensitive. Too slow.

But Grandin saw the world differently.

Where others saw noise, she saw patterns.

Where others felt overwhelmed, she saw systems.

> *"I am different, not less."*
>
> Temple Grandin

She spent her life designing humane systems for slaughterhouses.

Because she could see what others couldn't:

That empathy wasn't weakness – it was **leverage.**

She didn't just fix the chaos.

She **redesigned** it.

Her mind worked like a blueprint.

She mapped flow. She removed friction.

She turned industrial violence into something quieter, safer, more precise.

That's real leverage:

Not brute force.

But **engineered clarity.**

Grandin didn't need approval.

She needed space to build.

She found her lane.

Then made it unignorable.

And that's the move.

You don't need to be louder to matter more.

You need to build a system that multiplies your mind –

Even when no one's watching.

Hype Music

"CRANES IN THE SKY" BY SOLANGE

"I tried to drink it away..I tried to dance it away..."

This isn't just a song.

It's a systems warning.

Solange names every way we try to outrun discomfort - distraction, overwork, consumption, numbing.

But the ache doesn't vanish. It **compounds.**

Round Four is about building something quieter.

Something that holds your weight – not hides it.

Something that makes space for your actual self to show up.

"Cranes in the Sky" isn't about sadness.

It's about alignment.

Because you can't build freedom on top of chaos.

Combo Move - My Systems Hit Without Me

When I was building GRAIN, I didn't just make assets.

I built **engines.**

- *A prompt library that lets me spin up messaging in minutes*
- *Use case templates that cut pitch time in half*
- *Internal tools that summarize, prep, and clean - without needing me in the loop*

These don't just save time.

They **compound.**

That's the difference between a good week and a *repeatable weapon.*

Bourdain could walk into a kitchen and smell what was off.

Gladwell could see the outlier and name the pattern.

You need to look at your calendar, your energy, your tools - and build something that throws harder without you.

Learn With Me - Building Workflows that Multiply You

Featuring:

Saron Yitbarek

Founder, **Disco**; *Software Engineer & Educator*

> *"The best tools don't just save you time. They give you space to think."*

Saron has trained thousands of developers - and helped countless non-technical people understand how systems create scale.

She emphasizes this: AI doesn't need to replace you to be powerful. It just needs to multiply your decisions. A great workflow doesn't automate everything. It automates the right things - so you can focus on what only you can do.

In this round, you're not building speed. You're building space.

Corner Insight → *Don't automate what drains you. Automate what dilutes you.*

Corner Talk - No More Freestyling

I used to freestyle everything.

Every meeting. Every deck. Every launch.

And I didn't realize it was killing my edge.

Because I was burning energy just getting into flow –

instead of *staying* in it.

So I stopped winging it.

I started designing for rhythm.

Now?

- My meetings follow a tested arc
- My carousels follow a story frame that converts
- My templates turn "where do I start?" into "done by lunch"
- My days are anchored in output – not guesswork

This isn't rigidity. It's **creative freedom bought by frictionless design.**

When the system carries the weight, your mind stays free to fight.

Underdog Blood - From My Mom

I didn't grow up around Silicon Valley playbooks.

I grew up around **Chicago grit.**

My mom was raised in the city – tough as they come.

She lost her first son – my brother – to leukemia when he was eight.

On Mother's Day.

But she kept showing up. Every day after that.

That's what shaped me.

That's where the underdog spirit comes from.

The Stoic in me was born from watching her make peace with pain – and still fight forward.

That's why I don't waste time.

That's why I build systems that work in the dark.

Because every day matters.

The Finish - Leverage Lives in the Setup

> *"We don't rise to the level of our expectations, we fall to the level of our training."*
>
> Archilochus

This round isn't sexy.

It's not about going viral or dropping a mic.

It's about **architecture.**

The kind your future self will thank you for.

The kind that turns chaos into clarity.

The kind that frees you to **think bigger** - because the groundwork is done.

You don't need to grind harder.

You need to build something that **punches for you.**

Which output in my life currently requires the most effort per unit of impact - and how can I invert that ratio?

ROUND FIVE: FIND THE SIGNAL

Say Less. Mean More.

"The master's tools will never dismantle the master's house."

Audre Lorde

Bell Rings - You're Not Drowning in Work. You're Drowning in Noise.

You don't need more ideas.

You don't need more content.

You need **clarity.**

Because in the age of AI, **volume is cheap.**

Anyone can post ten times a day.

Anyone can hit "generate" and get twelve paragraphs of fluff.

Anyone can sound smart.

But can they be remembered?

Signal is what cuts through.

Everything else? Just static.

This round isn't about writing better.

It's about designing *impact* – messages that hit like a punch and stick like truth.

Training Camp - Content ≠ Signal

Most people confuse **output** with **clarity.**

They send more emails instead of saying what matters.

They generate pages instead of writing one sentence that lands.

They say "yes" to everything and end up communicating nothing.

AI didn't break communication.

It just exposed how many people were faking it.

You want trust?

You want traction?

You want momentum?

Sharpen the signal.

That means:

- *Say what you mean*
- *Cut what doesn't serve*
- *Design your message to land, not just exist*

Underdog Interlude - The Quiet Power of Emily Dickinson

Emily Dickinson barely left her home.

She rarely published.

She didn't chase platforms or attention.

And yet, 150 years later, her words still haunt us.

Her poems didn't yell.

They whispered.

They laced ordinary language with eerie precision.

She bent grammar.

She broke structure.

She distilled entire lifetimes into fragments.

> "Tell all the truth but tell it *slant.*"
>
> Emily Dickinson

While the world was busy posturing, she was pruning.

Every line. Every dash. Every silence was a design choice.

She wrote for the drawer.

But her signal was too sharp to stay hidden.

That's the thing about real clarity:

It doesn't need permission.

It doesn't need a stage.

It finds you. Cuts through. And lingers.

In a world chasing amplification, Dickinson chased exactness.

And she didn't just leave behind poems.

She left a blueprint:

Strip it down. ***Say it true.*** Let the silence do the rest.

Combo Move - The Signal Stack

Here's how I write, build, and communicate with clarity - even in chaos.

The Signal Stack:

Model → Use GPT, Claude, or Perplexity to brainstorm 10-20 messy ideas

Taste → Select the one that feels *true*, not just clever

Structure → Plug it into a tested framework (carousel arc, pitch, CTA)

Sharpen → Cut 70% of the first draft

Translate → Say it out loud. If it stumbles, slice again

That's how I write posts that punch.

That's how I build decks people remember.

That's how I wrote this book - **one sharpened signal at a time.**

Corner Talk - I Don't Publish Noise

In early 2025, I wrote a carousel that changed everything.

It didn't have the cleanest design.

It didn't have the flashiest hook.

But I rewrote it seventeen times.

I cut half the text.

I flipped the slide order the night before.

I swapped in a bell hooks quote.

And I deleted two examples I *loved* – because they weren't landing.

That post didn't go viral.

It went deep.

People messaged me a week later still thinking about it.

Friends forwarded it to their teams.

A director I admired told me it clarified something they'd been trying to say for months.

That's what signal does.

It doesn't shout.

It **lands in the gut – and stays there.**

"QUIETEST FRIEND" BY PEDRO THE LION

"...I didn't see it coming but now it's pretty clear / I traded my own wisdom for a jury of my peers."

This track doesn't explode - it unfolds.

Each lyric is a scalpel. Each chord, a slow exhale.

There's no clutter. No overproduction.

It's songwriting that **trusts the listener** to lean in.

That's what signal is:

The courage to be clear. The discipline to be still.

The craft of **saying less – so it lands harder.**

Put this on when your mind feels cluttered.

Then write like you're the quietest person in the room –

and still the one everyone hears.

The Finish - Say Less. Mean More.

> *"We must reject not only the stereotypes that others have of us but also those that we have of ourselves."*
> Shirley Chisholm

This isn't about branding.

It's about **identity – expressed with force.**

Sharpening your signal means

- Stop explaining. Start expressing.
- Stop performing. Start transmitting.
- Stop adding. Start cutting.

In a world of infinite noise,

the clearest voice wins.

What's one idea I've overcomplicated - and what would it sound like if I said it with perfect clarity?

ROUND SIX: WORK LIKE A TEAM OF TEN

You're not faking it. You're designing it.

"Don't wait around for other people to be happy for you. Any happiness you get you've got to make yourself."

Alice Walker

Bell Rings - You Can't Afford to Be the Whole Team

Still trying to do everything yourself?

Let me ask you:

Are your emails strategic?

Is your product evolving?

Is your content consistent?

Is your pipeline growing?

Is your personal life still intact?

Exactly.

You're not lazy.

You're not disorganized.

You're just still operating like a team of one in a world that demands you move like ten.

You don't need a bigger team.

You need a system with rhythm.

Achebe said stories don't belong to the loudest voice –

they belong to the one who understands the rhythm beneath the words.

In this world, rhythm is scale.

You don't need more hands.

You need a system that **moves like a squad** – and listens like a leader.

Training Camp - Build the Illusion of Scale

People assume scale means headcount.

Funding. Agencies. Infrastructure.

But the new leadership skill is **delegation through design.**

At GRAIN, I don't delegate to people.

I delegate to roles - powered by systems and AI.

That means:

- I don't write every word - GPT is my copy assistant
- I don't make every decision - AI summarizes tradeoffs
- I don't manage every detail - systems surface what matters

This isn't about cutting corners.

It's about **expanding surface area** without losing your edge.

Underdog Interlude - James Baldwin Never Worked Alone

James Baldwin was one man.

But when he wrote, it felt like a movement was speaking.

He didn't have a studio.

He didn't have a brand team.

He didn't have distribution.

What he had was force.

A voice sharpened by exile.

A rhythm formed by listening - deeply - before ever writing.

> *"You write in order to change the world... if you alter, even by a millimeter, the way people look at reality, then you can change it."*
>
> James Baldwin

Baldwin worked alone.

But he never sounded alone.

His writing moved like a team:

One part witness.

One part architect.

One part blade.

Every sentence carried strategy.

Every phrase did more than express – it *cut.*

That's the move.

You don't need a massive team to have massive reach.

You need clarity of voice.

You need discipline in rhythm.

You need a system of meaning so tight it echoes.

Baldwin didn't just write books.

He built machinery that dismantled lies – and delivered truth.

Work like a team of ten?

Start by crafting words that work harder than you do.

THE STRATEGIST *(Claude / GPT-4)*

- Frame problems
- Rephrase ideas for different audiences
- Suggest mental models or pivots

THE EDITOR *(GPT / Notion AI)*

- Polish first drafts
- Cut fluff
- Sharpen hooks and transitions

THE ASSISTANT *(Perplexity / Zapier)*

- Summarize docs
- Track workflows
- Pre-fill briefs, outlines, and next steps

THE DESIGNER *(Midjourney / Canva)*

- Rapid prototypes
- Explore brand style
- Build moodboards and pitch decks

Every tool is a role. Not a feature.

I don't just use AI.

I assign it.

Every system has a **lane.**

Every assistant has a **constraint.**

Together, they make me look 10x bigger - without adding a single headcount.

Learn With Me - Building Workflows that Multiply You

Featuring:

Dr. Rumman Chowdhury

CEO of Humane Intelligence & former Director of ML Ethics, Twitter

> *"We're moving from tools to teammates. And that shift demands intentional design."*

Dr. Rumman Chowdhury doesn't just build AI - she builds systems people can trust.

Her core insight?

AI won't organize your life. It will reflect your chaos - unless you lead it.

That means assigning roles. Defining boundaries. Knowing what your tools are for - and what they're not.

When you bring clarity, AI becomes more than a tool.

It becomes a teammate.

Corner Insight → *Don't just "use" AI.* ***Assign it. Align it. Direct it.*** *That's how you win.*

Corner Talk - You Can Still Own the Voice

Let me be clear:

I don't outsource my **taste.**

I don't automate my **art.**

I **direct.**

The biggest mistake people make is using these tools like magic.

They're not. They're **mirrors.**

They reflect what you feed them – then echo it back with velocity.

The power isn't in the prompt.

It's in your **intent.**

Every post. Every pitch. Every launch.

It's still *me* – but scaled.

Me, with infrastructure.

Me, without drag.

That's not cheating.

That's **craft.**

I'm still the walrus.

"THE GAMES WE PLAY" BY PUSHA T

"The only kingpin who ain't sinkin' / Chess moves are made, my third eye ain't blinkin'"

This isn't just a flex anthem.
It's a **blueprint for intentional motion.**

Every bar is lean. Tactical. Precise.

Just like a solo operator running tight systems with big reach.

Pusha doesn't shout.
He slices.

He doesn't explain.
He implies.

That's what it means to move like a team of ten:

- You're not louder. You're cleaner.
- You don't broadcast. You **transmit.**
- You don't hope it works. You **engineer** the impact.

Put this on when you're building systems that speak before you do.
When your output is proof.
When your presence is earned.

If you know, you know.

The Finish - You Are the Creative Director Now

> *"I'm deliberate and afraid of nothing."*
>
> Audre Lorde

You're not building a startup. You're building a **machine** that makes you unstoppable.

A machine that:

- Communicates on your behalf
- Preps you for the next decision
- Handles the first 80% of execution
- Never burns out, (almost) never forgets, never slows down

You're not faking it.

You're designing it.

And when people ask how you're doing so much?

Smile.

And say nothing.

Which part of my workflow still depends entirely on me - and how could I systematize it without losing quality?

ROUND SEVEN: CUT WITH PRECISION

You're Not Editing. You're Evolving.

"Beware the stories you read or tell; subtly, at night, beneath the waters of consciousness, they are altering your world."

Ben Okri

Bell Rings - You're Carrying a Ghost

There's a version of you that got you here.

The one who said yes to everything.

Held onto projects out of pride.

Protected fragile systems built in the dark and called them sacred.

That version was necessary.

But if you drag them forward now, they'll slow you down.

Maybe even stop you.

This round is about letting go.

Of identities.

Of rituals.

Of habits that once served you – but now dilute your edge.

You've built enough. You've proven enough.

Now you refine.

Training Camp - Focus Is the Sharpest Leverage

Most people think the hardest part of scaling is building.

It's not.

It's **cutting.**

- Projects you outgrew
- Channels that don't convert
- Calendar invites that reward presence over power
- Old versions of yourself you still feel loyal to

Your future doesn't care how hard you worked on the past.

This isn't minimalism.

This is **force protection.**

When you cut, you preserve.

When you cut, you focus.

When you cut, you send a signal:

I'm not here to maintain. I'm here to strike.

Underdog Interlude - Marie Kondo Was Never About Clean Rooms

Marie Kondo didn't just teach the world to fold shirts.

She taught it to *feel.*

People mocked her for asking if a sweater "sparked joy."

They missed the real message:

She was asking people to decide with integrity.

To cut with precision.

To honor the past without clinging to it.

To keep only what compounds your energy.

> *"The question of what you want to own is actually the question of how you want to live your life."*
>
> Marie Kondo

Kondo came from outside the Western productivity machine.

No hustle. No hacks.

Just deliberate practice.

Soft voice. Sharp blade.

That's what made her dangerous.

She didn't just clear space on your shelf.

She cleared space in your mind.

And in doing so, she made millions rethink what it means to choose.

This isn't about tidiness.

It's about **self-respect at scale.**

You want to work like a weapon?

Start by honoring your edge enough to cut what dulls it.

Combo Move - The 3-Question Knife

Here's how I decide what stays and what gets cut:

1. Does this compound my clarity or dilute it?

If it creates more questions than momentum, it's gone.

2. Would I build it again today?

If not, it's dead weight.

3. Am I keeping it out of loyalty or impact?

If I once loved it, I let it go with respect - not regret.

This isn't about optimizing everything.

It's about protecting the signal.

Every clean cut makes you sharper.

Corner Talk - I Deleted 40 Songs

During the pandemic, I wrote 40 songs for an album I never released.

Some we solid. A few were great. But none felt true.

They sounded like someone trying to be heard - not someone with something to say.

So I deleted the whole folder. No backups. Just gone.

The next song I wrote scared me.

It didn't sound right - it sounded *real.*

> *"I have to destroy what I've made in order to make the next thing."*
>
> Annie Clark (St. Vincent)

That's when I learned:

Cutting isn't loss. It's evolution.

"No Machine" by Adrianne Lenker

"Let no machine / eat away our dream"

This isn't just a song. It's a quiet refusal.

A soft, unwavering **no** to everything that feels artificial.

"No Machine" cuts away the scaffolding, the stories, the speed -

until only the essential remains.

Every strum is a clean break. Every lyric, a blade without malice.

This is music for shedding.

For stepping out of the role you once clung to.

For choosing presence over performance.

Put this on when you're letting go of systems, roles, and rituals

that once carried you - but no longer define you.

The Finish - You're Not Editing. You're Evolving.

"What you don't let go of is killing you slowly."
Chimamanda Ngozi Adichie

This isn't streamlining.

It's **sovereignty.**

You're not here to protect what used to work.

You're here to make room for what can.

Because impact doesn't live in clutter.

It lives in compression.

If it doesn't move you,

If it doesn't multiply you,

If it doesn't matter –

Cut it.

What story, system, or identity am I still carrying that no longer serves the version of me I'm becoming?

ROUND EIGHT: MAKE YOUR PRESENCE FELT

You don't rise to the occasion. You design it.

"**I'll tell you what freedom is to me:** ***no fear.***"

Nina Simone

Bell Rings - Make Your Presence Felt

This isn't about shouting.

It's about showing up so deliberately, you can't be ignored.

The most powerful rounds aren't always won with brute force.

Sometimes they're won with rhythm. With timing. With presence.

Most people confuse presence with performance.

They wing it.

They scramble in, hoping adrenaline will carry them.

That's not confidence.

That's chaos in a costume.

You've felt this cycle:

High output → *burnout*

Breakthrough → *collapse*

Spark → *drift*

And still – every time – you start from scratch.

You don't need more energy.

You need a **system for presence.**

Underdog Interlude - Claude Cahun Fought the Nazis with Performance Art

Claude Cahun didn't just show up.

They staged **presence as resistance.**

Photographer, writer, and surrealist saboteur –

they weaponized ambiguity in a time of uniformity.

In Nazi-occupied Jersey, Cahun and their partner Marcel Moore printed anti-German manifestos.

But they didn't sign them.

They **styled** them.

Slipped them into soldiers' pockets.

Pinned them to monuments.

Made every word feel like a whisper from a ghost.

> *"Under this mask, another mask. I will never be finished removing all these faces."*
>
> Claude Cahun

Cahun knew the truth:

Presence is power.

But not the kind measured in volume.

The kind that *unsettles, disorients, awakens.*

They blurred gender.

Bent reality.

And broadcast a message louder than any headline:

YOU WILL NOT ERASE ME.

That's what it means to make your presence felt:

To design your moment so intentionally it echoes in the bones of the room –

whether you speak or not.

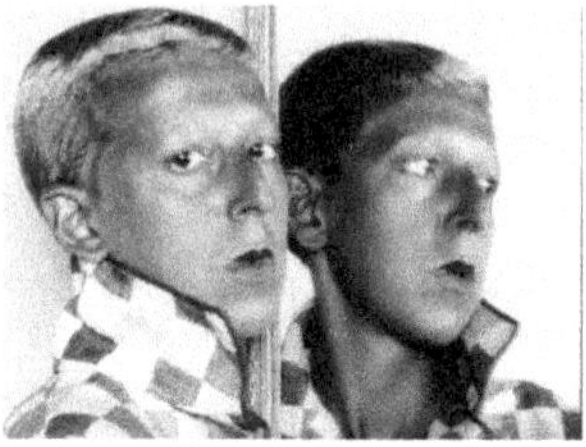

Claude Cahun

Experiment - The Blazer Phase

I live life like a science experiment.

Earlier this year, that mindset led to a shift that helped put me on the path to writing this book.

It wasn't groundbreaking.

But it may have been game-changing.

I started wearing blazers.

I started showing up early – **6:30 AM**, consistently.

Not for approval.

For data.

I tracked what changed:

- How people greeted me
- Who looped me in early
- What conversations I was suddenly invited to

Did the blazer matter? Not really.

But the **intent** did.

The **ritual** did.

The **rhythm** of how I entered a room started shifting how people responded –

even when I said nothing.

Presence is posture.

Presence is pattern.

Presence is energy.

It's something you **design**, not something you *hope* they notice.

That experiment didn't define me.

But it unlocked something:

Presence is a lever. Not a label.

Takeaway: *Shake it up. Enter different. Dress like you already own the room. In a world addicted to patterns, a sharp pivot is power.*

(Law 6: Court attention at all costs.)

Training Camp - Repeatability is Presence

Professionals don't wing it.

They don't wait for the right vibe or perfect calendar slot.

They sit down and hit what's already teed up.

Because they've built the scaffolding:

- Morning blocks
- Preloaded prompts
- Rituals that trigger flow
- Constraints that kill friction

This isn't rigidity.

It's **presence, preloaded.**

You don't rise to the occasion.

You fall to the quality of your system.

Combo Move - My Setup Rituals

Here's how I make presence a system:

Morning notebook

10 minutes, handwritten. No screen. Anchor thought.

Punchlist System

3 "hits" per day. One creative. One leveraged. One ops.

Stacked Prompts

I reuse and evolve high-performing GPT/Claude prompts.

Tuesday AM Writing Block

Sacred. Carousels happen here - not when I "feel like it."

Slack-blocking

No messages until my primary task is complete. Period.

These aren't hacks.

They're rituals.

Designed. Refined. Repeated.

Corner Talk - Boredom Is a Weapon

Here's the lie:

`You always need to iterate. Optimize. Switch it up.`

But the best builders I know?

Deliberately boring. Relentlessly so.

They don't chase novelty.

They run the setup.

> *"Be steady and well-ordered in your life so that you can be fierce and original in your work."*
> Gustave Flaubert

Because the setup ships:

- Weekly content
- On-time launches
- Clear, consistent thinking

When you find your rhythm? You don't disrupt it.

You **honor** it.

You **protect** it.

You **repeat** it.

"EVERYTHING IN ITS RIGHT PLACE" BY RADIOHEAD

"Yesterday I woke up sucking a lemon..."

It's the machine warming up.

A ritual coming online.

Spare. Cold. Precise.

Nothing explodes - everything just clicks into place.

The discomfort is intentional.

The repetition, meditative.

The groove, mathematical.

This is **automation as art.**

Order as atmosphere.

Every synth stab resets the cycle.

Every loop is a chance to surrender control and move inside the structure.

Put this on when you stop chasing chaos –

and start **designing your presence.**

The Finish - Setup Is Self-Respect

> *"Being an artist means forever healing your own wounds and at the same time endlessly exposing them."*
>
> Annette Messager

This round isn't about speed.

It's about **certainty.**

A great setup gives you:

- A **runway**
- A **rhythm**
- A **home base in chaos**

And when you master it?

You don't just get more done.

You become dangerous - on demand.

What would it look like to build a setup so good - you could disappear for a week and still create impact?

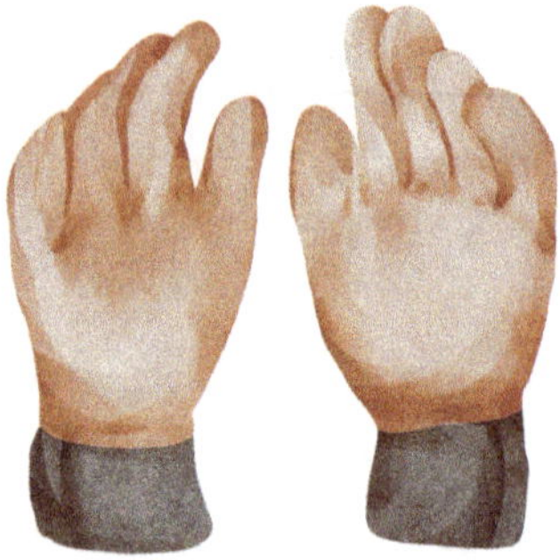

ROUND NINE: DROP THE SANDBAGS

You can't win carrying old weight.

"I am no longer accepting the things I cannot change. I am changing the things I cannot accept."

Angela Davis

Bell Rings - There's Someone You Need to Bury

In 2017, my mom died suddenly from a stroke.

She was a heavy smoker.

So was I.

That version of me – the one puffing through stress, sleepwalking through life, wearing armor I mistook for identity –

died with her.

Not instantly. But the countdown began.

The day of her funeral, I quit smoking cold turkey.

In the months that followed, I lost 100 pounds.

I started becoming someone she'd be proud of – if she were still here.

Somewhere between the sweat, the pain, the silence on those lakefront runs, I realized:

Letting go isn't weakness. It's reverence.

This round isn't just about change.

It's about honoring the transition.

Training Camp - You're Not Obligated to Stay Familiar

There's a version of you that fought to get here.

The overworker.

The people-pleaser.

The "always on" grinder.

The achiever who mistook exhaustion for proof of worth.

They served a purpose.

But they're not built for where you're going.

You don't need to resent them.

You don't need to defend them.

You just need to let them rest.

Growth isn't betrayal.

It's gratitude – with motion.

Combo Move - Audit the Armor

Transformation starts at the surface.

But it doesn't stop there.

When I began to truly evolve, I wasn't just shedding habits.

I was shedding identities:

"The guy who always says yes."

"The funny one who hides the pain."

"The one who's always available - no matter the cost."

My mom's death shattered the illusion that time is on layaway.

You don't get to keep borrowing presence.

You either **spend it** or **waste it.**

So I cut.

I stopped smoking.

Started running.

Chose my food. Protected my time. Respected my edge.

Not to feel better. But to survive better.

Corner Talk - The Best Builders Evolve Publicly

I didn't take a sabbatical.

I didn't go off-grid.

I built through the grief.

I posted through the shift.

I performed through the pain.

Because transformation isn't tidy.

It's not a rebrand. It's a reckoning.

But if you keep walking through the blur, something sacred happens:

The past stops chasing you.

The ghosts stay behind.

And the new version of you steps into the light – with nothing to hide and everything to offer.

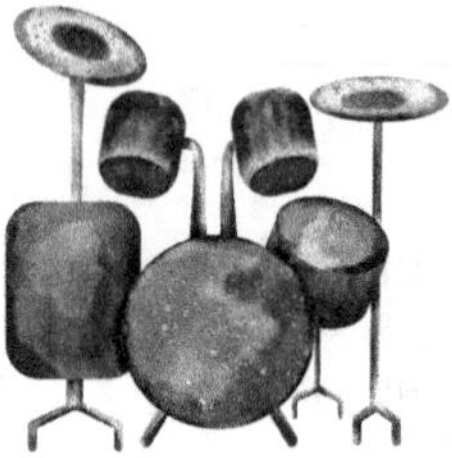

"LOVE AND DEATH" BY EBO TAYLOR

This isn't just a song – it's a procession.

Horn stabs cut through like memories you can't put down.

The rhythm moves forward, but never rushes.

It mourns. It grooves. It lets go.

Ebo Taylor's voice doesn't plead. It accepts.

The title tells the whole story: *you can't separate the two.*

"Love and Death" isn't just about grief - It's about carrying it with rhythm.

Letting the beat do what language can't.

It sounds like what happens when you drop the sandbags:

The tempo doesn't speed up. You just stop dragging ghosts.

This is the round where you bury the version of yourself that needed the weight.

Not in shame. In ceremony.

The Finish - Setup Is Self-Respect

> *"You have to act as if it were possible to radically transform the world. And you have to do it all the time."*
>
> Angela Davis

You don't owe allegiance to the version of you that survived the storm.

You owe it to the version that's ready to build the next one.

The old self fought.

Now let them rest.

Your new season demands:

- Less armor
- More alignment
- Less explaining
- More becoming

This round is a burial.

The next is a rebirth.

What belief about myself no longer holds up under scrutiny - and why am I still holding it?

ROUND TEN: PLAY OFFENSE, NOT DEFENSE

Build from your edge. Don't wait for permission.

"Freedom is not something that anybody can be given. Freedom is something people take."

James Baldwin

"RUNNING" BY HELADO NEGRO

A chill breeze in the middle of momentum.

This track doesn't lunge – it *glides.*

No explosion. No ego. Just forward motion, quiet and clear.

"You got me running, running, running... / just like you"

Each loop is a quiet refusal to stay stuck.

Each line, a breath of agency.

This isn't hustle music. It's *sovereign motion.*

The sound of moving when no one's watching.

Offense doesn't always yell.

Sometimes, it just doesn't wait.

Bell Rings - Stop Playing Cleanup Crew

If you're reacting to everything - every ping, every fire, every favor -

you're not in the fight.

You're in the audience.

Because here's the truth:

- Most calendars are defense.
- Most email is defense.
- Most meetings are defense.
- Most "busy work" is just proof you stopped leading.

Offense means deciding what matters - and hitting it before the world hijacks your focus.

This round is about **flipping the flow.**

Becoming the **initiator** again.

Taking the mic back.

On your own terms.

Underdog Interlude - Octavia Butler Didn't Wait to Be Chosen

Octavia Butler was rejected over 20 times.

Too speculative. Too Black. Too weird. Too bold.

She didn't yell.

She didn't plead.

She **persisted.**

Butler wrote herself into the future.

Literally.

She handwrote affirmations like spells:

> "I will find the way to do this. So be it! See to it."

Before the world caught up, she was already building worlds.

Worlds that weren't safe –

but *true.*

She didn't wait for an invitation to belong.

She designed the reality where she did.

> *"You don't start out writing good stuff. You start out writing crap. Thinking it's good stuff. And then gradually you get better at it."*
>
> Octavia Butler

That's offense.

Not performance.

Initiation.

Start when it's rough.

Move before it's validated.

Ship before it's perfect.

Butler didn't just play offense.

She made it **inevitable.**

Octavia Butler with a very photogenic horse

Training Camp - Defense Feels Safe. But It Doesn't Scale.

Reaction mode feels productive.

It makes you look essential.

But it's just inertia in disguise.

Defense keeps you in the game.

Offense changes the score.

The best builders don't wait:

- *They act.*
- *They publish.*
- *They lead.*

Then they log in.

Combo Move - Start the Day in Attack Mode

Here's how I stay on offense -

even while working inside a $20B org, even while building GRAIN on the side.

The Offense Stack:

- **Start screenless.**

I don't check messages until I name what matters.

- **Daily Lead List.**

Three people, ideas, or actions I want to spark today.

- **One outbound asset per week.**

A post. A pitch. A prototype. Something that initiates energy.

- **Calendar friction.**

If it doesn't serve offense, it doesn't get my best block.

This isn't about being cold.

It's about being in **control.**

Learn With Me - Build Teams That Multiply You

Featuring:

Amy C. Edmondson

Professor of Leadership and Management, **Harvard Business School**

> *"Psychological safety isn't a luxury – it's the birthplace of innovation and execution."*

Amy Edmondson is the world's foremost expert on psychological safety – a concept that underpins healthy, high-performing teams. A Harvard professor and author of *The Fearless Organization* and *Teaming*, her work shows that if people don't feel safe to speak up, even the strongest systems collapse.

Her approach?

Create environments where:

1. **Everyone speaks.** Silence kills both clarity and creativity.
2. **Failure is fuel.** Use mistakes to learn, not punish.
3. **Feedback is fluid.** Short loops, candid conversations.

She's researched and consulted across industries - from NASA to global healthcare - demonstrating that teams with psychological safety perform better, learn faster, and scale with sound judgment.

Her rule of thumb:

> "A team's ability to learn is the ultimate competitive advantage."

Corner Insight → *When your people feel safe, they challenge assumptions, share ideas, and step in early. That's how systems scale - not just in capacity, but in resilience and skill.*

Corner Talk - Proactive Energy Changes Everything

The shift to offense rewired me.

- I stopped waiting to be "ready." I posted what was true.
- I stopped hoarding ideas. I shared them early and watched them sharpen.
- I stopped waiting for permission. I started building evidence.

You don't need more confidence.

You need more data from your own courage.

And the fastest way to get it?

Make the first move.

The Finish - Don't Wait to Be Asked

> *"If you're silent about your pain, they'll kill you and say you enjoyed it."*
>
> Zora Neale Hurston

No one's going to say:

- "Now you can build."
- "Now you can lead."
- "Now you can post the truth."

You don't need that blessing.

You just need to move.

Make the ask.

Throw the punch.

Post the signal.

Ship the beta.

Book the meeting.

Break the mold.

This is your corner now.

Where in my life am I optimizing for safety instead of signal?

ROUND ELEVEN: BUILD YOUR CORNER

You don't need more tools. You need more truth.

"Surround yourself with people who are only going to lift you higher."

Oprah Winfrey

Bell Rings - You Can't Spar with Shadows

By now, you've built the system.

You've sharpened the signal.

You're landing clean punches.

But if you're still swinging alone, listen close:

Even champions don't train solo.

They build corners.

And corners aren't just fans.

They're not followers.

They're not the people clapping from the bleachers.

They're the ones lacing your gloves and telling you the truth.

A real corner:

- Challenges your plan, not your identity
- Sharpens your execution without dulling your spirit
- Respects your pace, but pushes your form
- Steps in when you're bleeding – and doesn't flinch

No matter how strong you are, you can't coach yourself between rounds.

Underdog Interlude - Miss Major Built Her Corner While the World Looked Away

Miss Major Griffin-Gracy didn't get platforms.

She got prison time.

She didn't get invites.

She got institutional abandonment.

Black. Trans. Poor. Incarcerated.

She had every reason to fold.

She didn't.

She built her own damn corner -

with zero blueprint and nothing but raw presence.

> *"I didn't have the luxury of quitting. Too many people needed to see me keep going."*
>
> Miss Major Griffin-Gracy

She mentored trans women inside prison walls.

Built community where the system left none.

Taught survival like gospel.

Not through slogans, but through staying.

Miss Major wasn't polished.

She was real.

She didn't coach from comfort.

She fought from experience.

And that's what a real corner does:

- *Loves you in the middle of the mess*
- *Prepares you for a world that doesn't care*
- *Doesn't need your perfection to protect your potential*

She wasn't mainstream.

She was *foundational.*

And for generations of underrepresented fighters, she still is.

The world may not give you a corner. Build it anyway.

Training Camp - People Are Systems, Too

You've systemized your time.

Your tools.

Your workflow.

Now it's time to **systemize your circle.**

Design it like a performance stack – because your inputs shape your outputs.

Here's the architecture:

THE STRATEGIST – *Sees angles you can't. Helps you zoom out when you're stuck in the weeds.*

THE SPARRING PARTNER – *Brings pressure. Points out sloppiness. Pushes you without ego.*

THE CORNER VOICE – *Speaks to your soul. Reminds you who you are when the noise gets loud.*

This isn't a boardroom.

This is your inner sanctum.

It might be:

- A friend who sends 90-second voice notes that land harder than any podcast
- A spouse who sees your drift before you do
- One person who won't let you coast, even when you're crushing it

You don't need a lot of people.

You need the right ones.

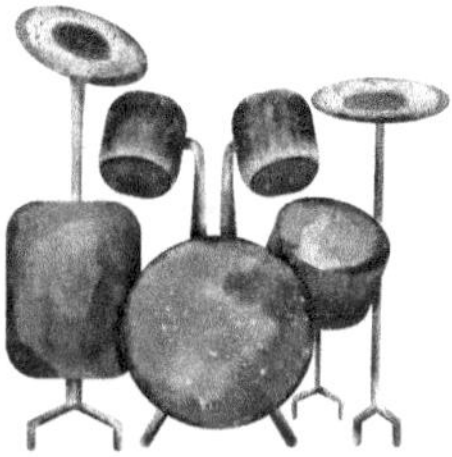

"ETERNAL LIGHT" BY FREE NATIONALS (FEAT. CHRONIXX)

This is not a war cry.
It's a frequency check.

"No bad vibes can stop this good vibration."

"Eternal Light" doesn't bang the door down.
It glows.
It vibrates with assurance, alignment, and selective energy.

It's not about hype – it's about harmony.
The kind of harmony you only feel when you're surrounded by the right people. The ones who match your rhythm. Sharpen your focus. Keep you grounded and lifted, both.

The groove is effortless. But the intention is loud:
Protect your peace.
Protect your people.
And don't let chaos anywhere near your signal.

Put this on when you're building your corner –
Not for noise, but for resonance.
Not to get loud, but to stay aligned.

Because the strongest corners don't yell.
They hum with eternal light.

Combo Move - Curate, Don't Collect

Here's who I've let go of:

- Group chats that became venting sessions
- Work friends bonded by complaints, not growth
- Mentors whose advice was rooted in fear, not faith

And here's who I've built with:

- My wife – a minimalist and creative force who cuts straight to truth
- My bandmates – who push my limits without letting me burn out
- One AI assistant – who never lets me lie to myself

That's my corner.

I don't reshuffle it when I get anxious.

I don't overcomplicate it when I feel alone.

Because I've learned:

Loyalty is earned.

But alignment is designed.

Corner Talk - Your Environment Is a Mirror

Want a glimpse of your trajectory?

Audit your inputs:

- The last 5 voices you let shape a decision
- The last 5 pieces of feedback you internalized
- The last 5 texts you replied to when you were depleted

That's your current corner – whether you chose it or not.

If they're not sharpening you, they're stalling you.

If they're not rooted in clarity and love, they're just background noise.

Build the team you'd trust to carry you when your legs go out.

Because the right corner won't let you shrink – even when you want to.

The Finish - Find People Who Won't Let You Shrink

> *"I show up for myself by choosing people who show up for me."*
>
> Alex Elle

This is the round where you stop soloing.

You've scaled yourself.

Now build the infrastructure that sustains you.

Find the voices that:

- Challenge your thinking without wounding your spirit
- Don't flinch when you're bleeding
- Refuse to let you forget what you're fighting for

This isn't weakness.

This is strategy.

This is architecture.

This is Round Eleven.

Next up?

You finish the fight.

If I could only take advice from three people for the next year - who earns that trust, and why?

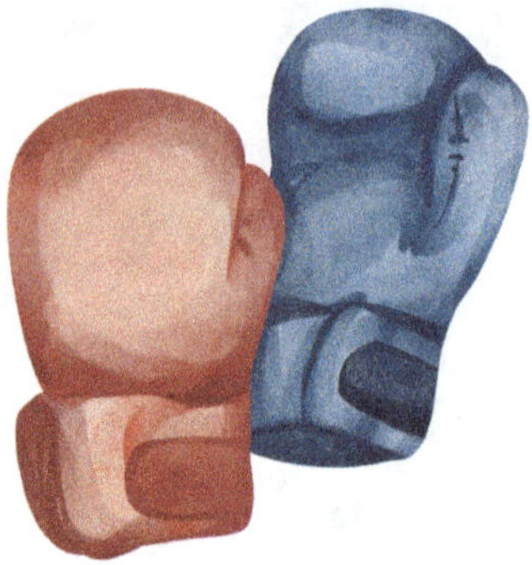

ROUND TWELVE: GO THE DISTANCE

Consistency wins what talent starts. Finish the damn fight.

"The road ahead will be long. Our climb will be steep. We may not get there in one year or even in one term – but America – I have never been more hopeful than I am tonight that we will get there."

Barack Obama, 2008

Bell Rings - Don't Let the System Win by Default

You know what happens to most people?

They build the system.

They do the reps.

They say the right things.

And then?

They hesitate.

They don't hit publish.

They don't send the proposal.

They don't pitch the idea.

They don't move.

They treat clarity like a mood instead of a mandate.

But clarity isn't something you wait for.

It's something you **act from.**

This round isn't about polishing.

It's about **finishing.**

Not when you feel ready.

But because you already trained for it.

Underdog Interlude - The Bears Have Always Been Built for the Long Game

You want to talk about going the distance?

Let's talk about Devin Hester.

It's 2007.

Super Bowl XLI.

First play of the game.

Everyone in America knows what's coming.

And they still can't stop him.

Hester fields the kickoff, stutter-steps, finds the seam.

Gone.

Touchdown.

The fastest six points in football history.

A spark from a city that was tired of waiting.

"That was for Chicago."

Devin Hester, postgame

That moment didn't end in a trophy.

But it did something else:

It reminded the world what this city is made of –

Resilience. Rhythm. Grit that doesn't flinch in the spotlight.

That's underdog energy.

Chicago energy.

And now?

The page is turning again.

Ben Johnson didn't have to take the job.

But he believed in this blueprint.

In this team.

In Caleb Williams – a quarterback wired for chaos, built for legacy.

This isn't hype.

This is infrastructure.

Chicago's not just chasing a championship.

We're building one. *please lord...*

From the locker room to the line of scrimmage –

This is what it looks like to finish the fight.

Training Camp - This Was Never About AI

You didn't come here to learn prompt engineering.

You came here to **reclaim momentum.**

Yes, the tools matter.

Yes, the systems help.

But none of it means a thing unless you move with conviction.

Conviction to hit send.

To go live.

To ask for what you want.

To say no to what doesn't serve.

To do **less**, but hit **harder**.

This was never about optimization.

This was about becoming **undeniable.**

Combo Move - The Punch You Haven't Thrown

Ask yourself:

What's the move I'm already trained to make - but still haven't?

The post.
The pitch.
The product.
The performance.
The uncomfortable call.
The overdue ask.

Write it down.
That's the punch.

Now throw it.

Don't crowdsource your courage.

Don't stall out waiting for more proof.

The signal's already in you.

The leverage is already built.

The reps are already logged.

You've earned the swing.

Corner Talk - Obama Didn't Wait to Be Perfect

You want to know what forward motion looks like?

It's Obama in 2008.

Not because he had every answer -

but because he moved with **voice**, **rhythm**, and **conviction**.

He didn't sell perfection.

He modeled action.

He gave people something even more powerful than hope:

Belief in their own motion.

That's what you owe the system you've built.

A chance to matter.

The Finish - You're Already the Person You Were Trying to Become

You didn't come here for a blueprint.

You came for a transformation.

And over twelve rounds, you've fought through:

- Identity fog
- Burnout cycles
- False starts
- Noise
- Shame
- Hesitation

And you've built:

- Rhythm
- Signal
- Systems
- Conviction
- Leverage

Now what?

Now you **finish.**

Not for applause.

Not for the algorithm.

Not for anyone else's validation.

But because you know who you are now.

And you know what matters.

The world doesn't need more people who hesitate.

It needs more people who move.

Who act like they've already been chosen – because they chose themselves.

Champ, you're out of rounds.

It's time to finish the fight.

Legacy Move - Ali Never Blinked

Before Ali was a legend, he was just a kid from Louisville with a mouth too big and hands too fast.

But he trained.

He planned.

He studied his opponents, exploited their rhythms, and stayed standing when no one else could.

He turned strategy into swagger.

Conviction into choreography.

Doubt into dust.

That was the blueprint.

Not just to fight – but to outthink, outlast, and outbelieve.

It was never about the knockout.

It was about knowing who you were, round after round, and refusing to blink.

That's what you've done here.

That's what it means to go the distance.

I keep a pair of autographed Ali and Frazier gloves on the tallest shelf in my studio.

That's where a champion's fists go after the final round.

Victory, earned.

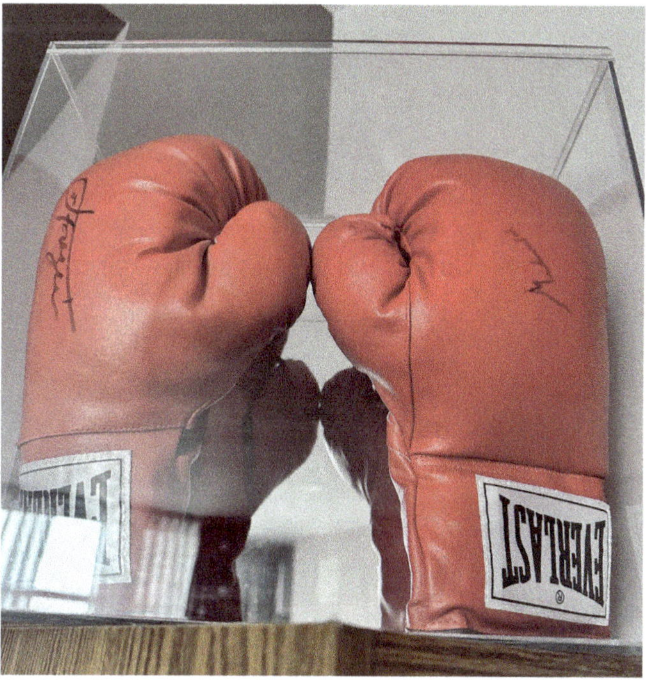

"A CHANGE IS GONNA COME" BY SAM COOKE

This isn't just a song.
It's a prophecy wrapped in pain.

Written after Sam Cooke was turned away from a whites-only motel,
this became the quiet anthem of anyone who kept **showing up**,
even when the world told them not to.

It's sorrow.
It's resistance.
But more than anything, it's **belief**.

Belief that the work means something.
That the effort counts.
That clarity cuts through.
That the fight is worth it - even when it's not fair.

You don't finish this round with noise.
You finish it with **truth**.

A voice that says:

Yes, the road is steep.
Yes, the fight is long.
But the change?

It's coming.

FINAL WORD

You made it to the end.

That says everything.

You built the system. You cut the noise.

You sharpened the signal.

You buried the old you.

You trained for impact. Now it's time to live like it.

Whatever comes next –

a launch, a leap, a reinvention,

or a quiet rebuild –

meet it with the grit of a fighter.

Not because life owes you anything.

But because you showed up **ready to earn it.**

"I am deliberate and afraid of nothing."
Audre Lorde

So keep swinging.

Stay sharp.

Stay dangerous.

Finish the fight.

– Ryan

GLOSSARY

Claude / GPT-4

Advanced large language models used for writing, ideation, and strategic thinking. Serve as co-pilots in problem framing, tone shifting, and mental modeling.

Notion AI

An AI assistant built into Notion. Great for polishing drafts, cutting fluff, and organizing thoughts during the writing process.

Perplexity

AI-powered research engine. Summarizes articles, answers questions, and helps with fast, source-backed exploration.

Zapier

A no-code automation tool that connects apps and triggers workflows. Great for moving data, sending alerts, and reducing manual busywork.

Midjourney

An AI image generator that creates visuals from text prompts. Used for prototyping brand assets, covers, and moodboards.

Canva

Design platform with drag-and-drop templates. Useful for building carousels, pitch decks, and visuals that punch above their weight.

Morning Notebook

A daily ritual – 10 minutes, handwritten. Used to center thoughts before screens take over.

Punchlist System

A 3-hit daily system: one creative, one leveraged, one operational. Keeps progress consistent without burnout.

Stacked Prompts

Pre-built prompt templates for AI tools. Saved and evolved over time to reduce friction and increase creative velocity.

Tuesday AM Writing Block

A sacred, non-negotiable space to write – especially LinkedIn content. Designed for flow, not force.

Slack-blocking

No incoming messages until your primary task is complete. A boundary ritual to stay in offensive mode.

Offense Stack

A system for moving first: screenless mornings, a lead list, one outbound asset per week, and calendar design with intention.

The Corner

Your personal board of directors. A system of relationships that challenge, sharpen, and steady you.

Ben Johnson

Now the Head Coach of the Chicago Bears. A creative offensive mind who finally gives this city the leadership it's been waiting for. The Ben + Caleb era begins.

Caleb Williams

The Bears' QB1. Not just built for speed - but for chaos, conviction, and big-stage clarity. Let's not put him in the Hall of Fame just yet. Give it 25 years.

ACKNOWLEDGEMENTS

To my mom – your loss lit the fire. I carry you with me in every word I write, every version of myself I outgrow. This book is for the version of me you believed in, even when I didn't see it yet.

To my dad – you're the reason I love boxing. We watched every Tyson fight in the '90s like it was sacred. I learned business by working for you. I learned grit by watching you. Your tenacity, presence, and discipline are woven through every chapter of this book. You didn't just teach me how to fight – you taught me how to last.

To my wife – your vision, precision, and presence keep me anchored. You don't just support me, you sharpen me. I wouldn't have the clarity or conviction to do any of this without your eye and your spirit. Thank you for always being in my corner.

To CJ & Jonathan, the other two members of Hunter-gatherer – thank you for challenging me creatively, relentlessly, and without ego. Our music isn't just sound – it's discipline, chemistry, and experimentation. You push me further, every time.

To my family – thank you for being my foundation, my fire, and my reason to keep showing up.

To Meshell Ndegeocello – the most underrated artist of our time. Thank you for your work, and for inspiring many of the quotes and music choices in the book (Audre Lorde and James Baldwin, to name a few).

To the readers – thank you for trusting me to speak into your momentum. I hope this book moves with you long after the last page.

To the Chicago Bears – for keeping me humble, hopeful, and just superstitious enough to believe this is our year. Caleb, Ben – bring this city the title it's been waiting for.

And to the machines – I asked a lot of you this week. You showed up. You held the mirror. You cut the fluff. Let's keep fighting above our weight.

– Ryan

ABOUT THE AUTHOR

Ryan J. Smith is a strategist, builder, and creative weapon for the AI age.

He's the founder of GRAIN, an infrastructure startup helping enterprises turn messy internal data into LLM-ready assets. By day, he leads AI product initiatives inside a $20B healthcare company. By night, he writes, performs, and builds systems designed to help ambitious people hit above their weight.

After losing his mother unexpectedly in 2017, Ryan overhauled his life – from smoking to sobriety, from chaos to clarity, from burnout to leverage. He's since built a career, mindset, and mission around helping others do the same.

He believes in scaling with intention, evolving in public, and always throwing the first punch.

Say less. Move smart. Stay dangerous.

ALSO BY

RYAN J. SMITH

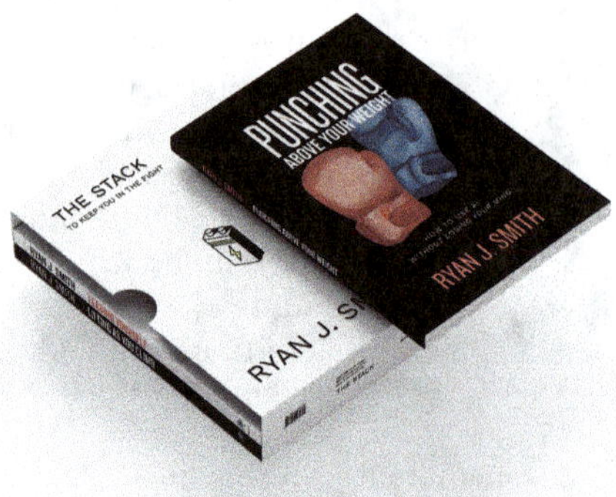

The Stack: To Keep You in the Fight (Volume I)

This book is part of The Stack – a focused collection built to help high-output humans stay grounded, sharp, and in motion. These aren't just books. They're tools. Fuel. Strategic hits of clarity to keep you in the ring.

Punching Above Your Weight

How to harness AI without losing your mind.

A tactical guide for working smarter, leading sharper, and scaling what actually matters.

Leading Yourself ***(Coming Soon)***

Before you lead a team, a company, or a mission – you have to lead your own damn self.

Mental clarity. Emotional discipline. Resilience on demand.

Lifting As You Climb ***(In Progress)***

For the ones building something bigger than themselves.

About mentorship, collaboration, and giving without breaking.

Stay Charged. Stay Strategic.

Subscribe for early releases, bonus chapters, and real-time field notes at:

ryanjeffreysmith.com

www.ingramcontent.com/pod-product-compliance
Lightning Source LLC
LaVergne TN
LVHW022210200926
848481LV00006B/1915
9798218705497